A Gospel Treasury

Poems Based on Lectionary Gospels
Cycle B

ANDREW DAUGHTERS

C.S.S. Publishing Co., Inc.

Lima, Ohio

A GOSPEL TREASURY B

Copyright © 1990 by
The C.S.S. Publishing Company, Inc.
Lima, Ohio

Library of Congress Cataloging-in-Publication Data

Daughters, Andrew, 1920-
    A Gospel treasury : poems based on lectionary Gospels, cycle B / by Andrew Daughters.
        p.   cm.
    ISBN 1-55673-253-8
    1. Bible. N.T. Gospels — History of Biblical events — Poetry.
2. Christian poetry, American.   I. Title.
PS3554.A855G6   1990
811'.54—dc20   90-1345
                                                                CIP

9041 / ISBN 1-55673-253-8   PRINTED IN U.S.A.

In Memory of John,
who went home first

How to Use This Book

You may use the poetry in this book in several ways:

• Read it for personal devotional enrichment. Read the appropriate selection before the Sunday for which you are next planning worship and preaching. In the tradition of personal journal-keeping, the content of the poetry here may prompt you to your own creation on the same text and theme.

• Use the poetry in your preaching, either to introduce, illustrate, or conclude the message. You may find that an every-Sunday usage is too frequent for your parish. On the other hand, the congregation may respond favorably enough so that you choose to make these poems every-Sunday features of your proclamations.

• Invite a lay reader to share the appropriate poem at a place in the worship service which you and/or the worship planning team decide is most fitting.

• Print the poem on a bulletin insert, or in your weekly newsletter (if you publish a weekly one). If this is done, the author and the publisher request that you provide a simple credit line, indicating the source.

Foreword

Delight! That is what most readers will experience when they first pick up Andrew Daughters' poetic commentary on the Gospels in the liturgical lectionary.

Since the late 1970s, when a burst of ecumenical sensitivity led many churches to cooperate in the production of a three-year lectionary cycle, hardly any preacher (or hearer of sermons) can complain of a too-limited selection of biblical references for homilies at Sunday worship. Indeed, in most lifetimes, the ready supply of homiletic material is inexhaustible. Such is the richness of our heritage.

The existence of the lectionary is a kind of protection for both listener and preacher alike in those congregations where the preacher has a commitment to regular preaching from the lectionary. For the listener the protection lies in not being at the mercy of some preachers who seem regularly to lift up one emphasis of Christian teaching at the expense of many others. For the preacher, it provides a balanced diet which can feed and stimulate his/her homiletic imagination.

Yet who among us who claim the privilege of communicating the Good News will not admit to those occasional dry spells, when nothing will suffice save the application of nutrients and moisture to our creativity? Sometimes humorous, sometimes terse, always compassionate, Andrew Daughters' (well-) versed commentary on the Gospels will fill this need beyond normal expectation.

But there is more. The transparent joy of knowing God in Christ, which friends have seen in Andrew Daughters' thirty-seven years of ordained ministry, is clearly visible in this book of simple verse. Clergy will quote from it in sermons or bulletins and, more important, glean new insight from familiar passages. Lay persons will find themselves introduced anew to the Lord of love. All will be warmed by the caring of the loving God revealed in these pages.

Don't stop here! Read on . . . and enjoy.

The Rt. Rev. George N. Hunt
Bishop of Rhode Island (Episcopal)

February 13, 1988

A Word About Lectionaries

The author has created this poetry resource for use with three lectionaries presently widely in use among mainline Christians, the Common (used by Episcopalians, United Methodists, and Presbyterians), the Lutheran, and the Roman Catholic. The Gospel texts used in these three lectionaries are almost always identical. There are cases where there are variations or divergences. In those cases, where the divergence is significant, an effort has been made to provide alternative material.

In rare cases the writer departs from the assigned Gospel text for a church day and uses an alternative which, nevertheless, speaks to the theme of the day. A case in point is the first alternative for Easter Day (The Resurrection of Our Lord).

In the second half of the church year (the "Sundays after Pentecost" or "Sundays in Ordinary Time") material is assigned to the three lectionaries in the following manner:

- The Common Lectionary follows the "Proper" designation;
- The Lutheran Lectionary follows the "Pentecost" designation;
- The Roman Catholic Lectionary follows the "Ordinary Time" designation.

Both Common and Roman Catholic lectionaries follow a date-specific pattern for locating Gospel texts in the second half of the church year. These dates appear at the top of each page. Lutherans merely follow the assigned Sundays after Pentecost.

About the Author

The Rev. Andrew Daughters is the son of a pioneer missionary of the Episcopal Church in the west who served congregations in Washington, Idaho, Oregon and Montana. His mother, a native Washingtonian, bequeathed to Andrew a love of poetry and his father gave him a love of the church. These he has combined in the present work.

After farming for eight years after college, during which time he married his college sweetheart, Carleen, and started a family, Andrew left the farm and went into the ordained ministry. During the years after ordination, he has been a part of the building of one church structure, two parish halls and the remodeling of two other church buildings. He has also built two homes for himself and his family. He lives at present in one of them. He has also brought three small mission churches to the stage where they were self supporting parishes. He and Carleen have given birth to four sons in the forty-five years of their life together.

Andrew started writing at an early age but did not take it seriously until in retirement, when he set himself to write at least one poem for each Gospel in the three year Common lectionary. He now finds himself writing almost every day. His style is determined by the fact that poetry to be used in sermons must be understood at first hearing or it is lost. These poems have also been used on bulletins and inserts, and have been found to be a good way of getting the congregation to take the bulletins home rather than leave them to be picked up after services. He decided to seek publication at the encouragement of members of his congregation.

Advent 1
Mark 13:32-37

Through the ages men have wondered,
talked about the end of time.
Some have said they had the answers
with a formula divine.
But we cannot know the answers
nor perceive the how or when.
We can hardly know the questions;
it's so far beyond our ken.

What will close the human era?
How will end our little tale?
Will it come in fire and thunder?
Will the mushroom cloud prevail?
Will it be a bolt from heaven
that ignites the holocaust?
Or will earthly fools demolish
all the good that will be lost?

Will the works of man be covered
by the jungles and the dust,
then to be amalgamated
into earth's absorbing crust?
Will it be Creation's ending
when the day of man is done?
Or will man be soon forgotten
as the rest of life goes on?

There's a thought intrigues me more
than when the end of time will be.
What concerns me more than that is,
"When will be the end of me?"
That I do not know the timing
hardly bothers me a bit.
I'll just leave it in the hands
of Him who started all of it.

Advent 2
Mark 1:1-8

Long ago Isaiah said it,
prophesied a messenger
who would come before Messiah
acting as his harbinger.

Last of prophets, first of martyrs,
John fulfilled his given role,
calling men to their repentance
so that God could make them whole.

John prepared all those who'd hear him
as Isaiah had forseen.
He baptized them in the Jordan
to denote that they were clean.

and he warned that the Messiah
soon would make his presence known.
And, fulfilling God's intention,
he would come to claim his own.

John said, "Now's the time appointed.
Waiting time is almost done.
Make yourselves a fitting people
to receive the Holy One."

John still calls us to repentance
so that God can set us free
from a life without a purpose,
from our ways of apathy.

In the deserts of our lives, we
still need help. We still are lost.
So prepare yourselves to greet him
who will save, whate'er the cost.

Advent 3
John 1:6-8, 19-28

There are many men seek power
and pursue it all their lives,
while another man seeks glory
and for it he always strives.
For John, Baptizer, neither one
was what in life he sought.
'Twas shown by what he practiced
just as well as what he taught.

Out in the wilderness he called
the people to repent.
To make a way for God to come
he said that he was sent.
And he called men to the Jordan,
there to listen and to pray
as they confessed and asked the Lord
to wash their sins away.

"I am really not Messiah.
That's what I have always said.
No, nor yet am I Elijah,
now arisen from the dead.

I am simply here to witness
to the light that is to come,
and to call men to repentance
that God's holy will be done."

As I think of the Baptizer
and his working in his time,
It occurs to me that one thing
makes his life seem so sublime.
And there's one thing I have learned
from John in contemplating fame:
'Twas his lack of seeking glory
that brought glory to his name.

"I am not the Lord's Anointed.
I can but prepare his way.
Soon will come the time appointed.
He will come without delay."

John, when asked, "Are you Messiah?"
disavowed the holy claim,
bade them hold their hallelujah
till the true Messiah came.

Many followed John until the
time when Jesus later came.
He it was who would fulfill the
prophecy and gain the fame.

Soon the followers of John
in multitudes began to leave.
Some who saw it might imagine
John would agonize and grieve.

When he saw them go to Jesus,
John said, "Jesus must increase.
He, the Bridegroom, now is with us.
I in turn will now decrease."

We, like John, are called to witness
to the Lord of love we know.
Unlike John, we're often speechless
when the proper moments show.

Are we filled with apprehension,
fear that we will be outshone?
Would we rather gain attention
pointing to ourselves alone?

Advent 4
Luke 1:26-38

Ann's daughter, Mary,
had a great vision:
a messenger angel,
bearing a promise.
She wondered just what it could mean.

Then, pregnancy started,
to visit a cousin,
beginning her task to believe,
said she with emotion,
"My soul must proclaim
the greatness of God.
My spirit rejoices in glory.
He has visited me with His almighty favor
and people will all call me blest.

Lord, what was the blessing you gave her?
A journey to Bethlehem town,
heavy with child,
no room at the inn,
a cowpen her lying-in room,

her cradle, a manger,
while overhead, angels
gave praise for the night.

And so Mary pondered.
She pondered and wondered.
She pondered all this in her heart.

And this was the blessing,
the God-given blessing
that Mary, that night did receive:
The hands and the feet and the side of her baby
were scarless and lovely to see.

Her blessing that night was not knowing the future.
Not knowing was blessing enough.

Christmas Day
Luke 2:1-20

Love to us at Christmas came
to live with us on earth.
Jesus was the infant's name
and humble was his birth.

For in a manger he was laid,
so cold and dark the night.
Yet o'er his birthplace angels prayed,
rejoicing at the sight.

All praise and love to God on high
and on the earth be peace.
Good will to men, the angels cry.
God's love will never cease.

The child whose birth we celebrate
now rules the earth in love.
And he has opened wide the gate
for us to heaven above.

O, Love of God in human form,
you bring us joy and healing.
You came, your mercies to perform,
the Father's love revealing.

Christmas Day

(Roman Catholic)
Luke 2:15-20

What a night of great excitement!
(Shepherds lead a quiet life.
Barring wolf or bear incursion,
they have little thrill or strife.)
Yet, upon the night I speak of,
angel voices they had heard
telling them in wondrous phrases
that a great thing had occurred.

They were told that, as they listened,
in the town of Bethlehem,
there was born the great Messiah.
And a sign was given them.
They would find him in a manger,
Lying wrapped in swathing bands.
He was sent to save his people
by a God who understands.

Shepherds then had gone to seek him,
found the child as they were told.
He, "The One Who was to Come,"
their eyes were priv'leged to behold.
And their ears had heard the chorus
angels sang for all their worth
praising God's eternal glory,
singing peace to men on earth.

Shepherds too, had joined the singing
as, returning to their sheep,
they had praised the God of glory.
After all, how could they sleep?
Through the ages, saints have echoed
with their lives the angel song.
It's the everlasting theme song
of the church where we belong.

Christmas 1
Luke 2:22-40

Rejoice! To us a child is born.
Behold, a son is given.
We hail a new beginning
as we celebrate our hope.

And yet, how little human eyes can see,
for here, amid our great festivity,
if we but lift our eyes,
across the years,
a cross appears,
a scourge,
a crown of thorns
and death.

Be thankful Mary could not see
beyond what was, what was to be.
She'd see him grow
yet could not know
that he would pay with life
for human sin
and die
that we might live.

O, Almighty One, I pray
that in our hearts today,
we're not enticed
to see the Christ
as babe alone.
Let it be known
that this is He
who sets us free
eternally.

Christmas 1 or Christmas 2

(Episcopal)

John 1:1-18

In the beginning,
Before the beginning,
Within all beginning,
To cause all beginning,
Was God.

At work in creation,
In joy and elation
To share His relation
With God in creation,
Was Christ.

'Twas God who first knew him.
All things were made through him.
All reverence is due him.
So bow the knee to him,
The Christ.

The Lord, uncreated,
By love animated,
To peace dedicated,
In hope unabated,
The Christ.

From heaven progressing,
All power possessing,
Transgression addressing,
Forgiveness expressing
Is Christ.

The light he projected,
The darkness rejected.
The love he reflected
Still glows, now perfected.
In Christ.

Christmas 2 or Feast of the Epiphany

(Episcopal)

Matthew 2:1-12

Through the night it shone afar,
shone the strange and brilliant star.
Travelling with laden beast,
came the strangers from the east,
came to seek the infant there,
bringing precious gifts and rare.

Through the desert, on they came,
seeking him of Holy Name.
Westward to Jerusalem,
southward then to Bethlehem,
seeking him, the infant king,
seeking still their gifts to bring.

Christmas 2 or Feast of the Epiphany

(Episcopal)

Matthew 2:1-12

When they found the holy child
and his mother, undefiled,
there they laid their treasures down.
Gold for shaping him a crown,
incense for an odor sweet,
myrrh, they offered at his feet.

Comes Epiphany again.
We who recognize his reign
also offer gifts most rare,
offer him our lives to share.
So when time on earth is done,
Life with him has just begun.

Epiphany 1
Mark 1:4-11

John went into the wilderness
and there began to preach.
Multitudes came out to him.
Repentance did he teach.
From all Judea they went out
to see this man of God.
All girdled round with camel skin
he must have looked quite odd.

Said John, "With water I baptize
to take away all sin
and lift the burden from your back
so new life can begin.
There will be one, come after me,
whose shoes I can't unlace.
He'll baptize you with Spirit and
you'll meet God face to face."

Then came a strange and wondrous thing
for Jesus came to John
and asked to be baptized by him.
The day was nearly gone.

But, as into the stream he went,
the heavens opened wide.
And Spirit, as a dove came down
and flew there at his side.
And echoing, a voice was heard
as God the moment seized.
"Thou art my well-beloved Son
in whom I am well pleased."

What happened there to Jesus, friends,
has also come to you.
For you are called, as Jesus was,
to learn God's will to do.
And we can walk at Jesus' side.
He'll be our guide and stay.
For he's our elder brother
and he's with us all the way.

Epiphany 2
John 1:35-42

Glorioski, come and see!
Mom and dad bought me a horse
and, because you're close to me,
you can ride him, too, of course.

What a most astounding day!
Dad gave me a new Corvette.
Others watch in green dismay,
Greatest status symbol yet.

Won't you come and visit us?
See our brand new residence.
We won't make a lot of fuss.
I've arrived. Here's evidence.

Share the wonder that is mine.
We now have a ten-pound boy.
Mom and son are doing fine.
What a time of pride and joy.

Andrew, in excitement ran
to his brother, Peter, where
he gave word of God with man.
That was news he had to share.

"Brother, we have seen the light.
We have found our God's Messiah.
Now the future all looks bright.
Share with us an Alleluia."

Why do we so soon declare
passing glories that befall?
Yet we rarely ever share
Christ, the greatest gift of all.

Epiphany 2

(Episcopal and Lutheran)

John 1:43-51

"Can anything good come from Nazareth?"
was the question Nathaniel framed.
And the question said less about Nazareth
than it did of the gentleman named.

Our origins are less important
than the things that we say and we do.
And sometimes from unlikely sources
come gifts that are lovely and true.

While silk purse does not come from sow's ear,
as grandmother said. Never will.
It comes from a source as unlikely,
from a worm that is uglier still.

So be sure to check out your assumptions
to see if they really are true.
If your prejudice leads you to label,
then your labelling may label you.

"Come and follow me," said Jesus
to the men beside the sea.
And they left their nets and followed
from the shores of Galilee.
"Come and follow me" to Matthew
at the tax collector's table,
And he left accounts and money
just as fast as he was able.
Come and follow me, says Jesus,
come and follow me today.
I will set you free, says Jesus.
Come and follow while you may.

And what does it mean to follow him?
To walk with him, to stay with him?
It means to begin to think with him,
to see with him, to pray with him,
to see the world as it is with him,
to find ourselves growing in love with him
and through all our lives to give with him.
It means to be able to share with him,
to be sad with him, to have fun with him,
To be glad we will never be done with him
and then, at the end to be one with him.

Epiphany 4
Mark 1:21-28

When Jesus sent the demon out
and bade him go away,
he freed the man in whom he dwelt
from sin and disarray.

For there in old Capernaum
he taught a mighty fact.
Where Jesus Christ is fully known,
Sin is not free to act.

Most loving Lord, now hear our prayer.
Erase our sin and doubt.
And help us with your mighty pow'r,
to cast our demons out.

And give us grace to let them go,
familiar though they be,
and take your place within our lives
throughout eternity.

When Jesus came to Peter's house,
his moth'r-in-law was sick.
Jesus waited not for others.
He was confident and quick.

He took her by the hand and,
as she rose up from the bed,
she found her illness leaving
and her fever, too, had fled.

Thus restored, she came to serve him
and was diligent indeed,
out of gratitude to help him
and to meet his every need.

When Jesus comes to my house
and he cures my life of sin,
will I be quick to serve him?
Or will I, to my chagrin,

Find I quickly have forgotten
how, in love, he set me free,
as again I get distracted
by the world surrounding me?

Lord, as you have cured my fever,
help me now to sing your praise.
Grant that, filled with loving kindness,
I may serve you all my days.

Epiphany 6 • Proper 1
Mark 1:40-45

A leper came to Jesus,
a living man, yet dead.
He asked the Lord to cleanse him.
"If you will, you can," he said.
And Jesus said, "I will it."
and drove him not away.
Then, touching the untouchable,
he stopped the dread decay.

"See to it," Jesus told him,
"You tell no man at all.
But go and show the priest
that you have no mark or gall.
so he can certify you
that leprosy is gone.
Then make the gift that Moses claimed,
and lo, it all is done."

The leper left, rejoicing
and telling of his cure.
For how could he keep quiet
now that his skin was pure?

He had to tell the story,
how Jesus made him sound.
He could not cease the telling,
but spread the news around.

Now I can just imagine
the joy he must have known
as once again he entered
the place that was his own.
Again with friends and family,
no longer they would mourn.
For he, once dead, was living
as though he'd been reborn.

Lord, if I ever wonder
how far your hand can reach,
remind me of that leper
and all that he could teach.
For, touching the untouchable,
you cured and made him whole
and showed how far you'd stretch your hand
to save a human soul.

Epiphany 7 • Proper 2
Mark 2:1-12

Four men came to Jesus,
came bringing a friend
who was paralyzed. He could not walk.
But they could not come close for
so great was the crowd
who were gathered there hearing him talk.

So the friends, getting desperate,
went to the roof
where they opened a hole overhead.
Then, attaching some ropes
to the mat where he lay,
they let down their friend on his bed.

When the Lord saw the faith
that their actions portrayed,
he took pity upon the poor soul.
He forgave him his sins
and then bade him arise,
in both body and spirit made whole.

As I read, I remember
how many poor souls
I have known who had just such a need
for such friends as were there
who would work to be sure
he was brought to the Lord to be freed.

And one last little note
as I think once again
how this paralyzed man was restored:
What a love those friends had
to be raising the roof
to be sure that their friend met the Lord!

Epiphany 8 • Proper 3
Mark 2:18-22

There are times and there are seasons
and God only knows the reasons
our existence seems to wander up and down.
For our lives have variations,
sorry times and celebrations,
times you feel like you're a hero or a clown.

Every feeling God has given
us to use while we are livin'
we will need some time or other in our lives.
There will be a time for sighing,
even be a time for crying.
That's a certainty, no matter how one strives.

There'll be times when you'll be smiling,
times when life will be beguiling,
when you feel like you're a winner all the way.
Then again, when life's abusing
you, you'll feel as though you're losing,
times the piper seems to ask for double pay.

So be honest with your feeling.
For the stoic's not appealing.
And the difference 'twixt a robot and a man
is that people give expression
to elation and depression:
and we're all that way from king to courtesan.

Then, whatever be your purview,
when the one you love is with you,
celebrate his presence now, while he is here.
For the time may come tomorrow
to express the deepest sorrow
as you're weeping at the loss of all that's dear.

Transfiguration • Lent 2

(Roman Catholic)

Mark 9:2-9

From out the cloud that wrapped them round
there came to them an awesome sound
for, when the solemn silence broke,
the voice they heard was God, who spoke
and said, "This is my chosen son.
Hear him."

When we are with him on the mount
as, contemplating the account
we have of what took place that day,
'twill likely make us want to stay
As long as life on earth shall run,
near him.

But life's not always so sublime
nor always lived on "mountain time."
His words then help us find the key,
"Take up your cross and follow me."
If life you'd have with nought but fun,
Fear him.

In this life, he's our guide and strength.
and, when we face our death at length,
he'll sit in judgment on our lives;
from him our hope of heav'n derives.
Through him eternity is won.
Revere him.

Lent 1
Mark 1:9-15

Lord, I pray
every day,
"Lead us not into temptation."
I have heard
that same word
practically from my creation.

Yet, I vow,
still somehow,
much temptation seems to find me.
And I fall.
I recall.
There's no need, Lord to remind me.

Why me, Lord?
Are you bored?
Do you have a grudge against me?
Tell me straight.
Is it bait?
Are you only out to test me?

What's that, God?
Now that's odd.
You say, Jesus, too, was tempted.
It sufficed
Jesus Christ?
Even he was not exempted?

Maybe, God,
it's not odd.
Maybe it could be no other.
I'm restored
to my Lord
through the Christ, my elder brother.

Help me, Lord.
Say the word.
You know all about temptation.
Help me bear.
Help me share.
Lead me into your salvation.

Lent 2
Mark 8:31-38

"Don't speak of death," said Peter
as he took the Lord aside.
"Don't even think about it.
It's a thought I can't abide.
If you should die tomorrow
then your movement would be dead.
And think what would become of us.
It fills my heart with dread.

"Your church is much too feeble,
just a pitiable few.
We must have many thousands
and it all depends on you.
How can you be Messiah
if your death is premature?
You must gather men and power
for your kingdom to endure."

Like Peter, we so often think
the church's power depends,
like human institutions, on
its wealth and numbers, friends.
But no! The church goes forward,
not by human strategem,
Just two or three may gather
and the Lord is there with them.

So pick your crosses up, my friends
and join the march sublime.
Our task is just to change the world,
one mortal at a time,
to change the hearts of people,
not just changing their facade.
The task is hard. But we'll succeed.
We have the help of God.

Lent 3
John 2:13-22

A space for God,
I need a space to set aside,
a room to prepare,
a meeting house,
a tent of meeting,
a tabernacle, a chapel of the soul,
a cathedral of the spirit.

And yet . . .
The God of space requires no space to be,
the Lord of all creation, no created home.
The Lord of many mansions needs no earthly room.
And I may be confronted by him on any road,
whether from Jerusalem to Jericho
or backstreet Bethlehem
or Fourth Street, U.S.A.

Who then needs shelter? Is it he
whose shelt'ring wings I seek so oft in fear?
Or is it I, who cringe beneath life's burdens,
bent low with aching back?

O Holy, Saving One,
help me to know that it is not your need
I would assuage, but mine.
And help me know that you alone
are home enough for me
for now
and for eternity,
and, stranger still, to know
that I myself am a temple for you.

Lent 4
John 3:14-21

God's love is like a gentle breeze
that cools my fevered brow.
It teaches me to be at ease
and worries won't allow.

God's love is like a whirlwind
that sweeps me off my feet
and shakes me up when I have sinned,
then brings me rest complete.

God's love is like a burning flame
that lights my darkened room
to show the way and sight reclaim,
to drive away the gloom.

God's love is like a restless sea,
as powerful and strong.
At times it washes over me
to move my faith along.

God's love is like a mighty wave.
Relentlessly it moves,
humanity at last to save
and all our lives improve.

God's love is constant as the tide,
refreshing as the spring.
For each of us, down deep inside,
God's love is everything.

God's love is really much much more
than all our similies.
No thoughts expressed in human lore
reach God's realities.

God's love is indescribable;
that cannot be denied,
and my loss inexpressible
if I had never tried.

Lent 5
John 12:20-33

A group of Gentiles came to Phillip.
Greeks they were,
sincere, earnest men, God-seekers.
"We would see Jesus, Sir," they said.
What had they heard of him?
What did they know?
What did they want of him?
What was their need?

Over the years,
as we look back,
we think,
"How fortunate to see the Lord,
to see his smile,
to hear his voice,
to touch his hand."

Jesus said, "He who has fed the hungry,
clothed the naked, welcomed the stranger,
visited the sick and imprisoned,
has fed, clothed and welcomed me,
has visited me.

Would you see Jesus?
Go to the prisons, visit the sick,
feed the hungry, clothe the naked.
From each emaciated face,
the eyes of Jesus look on you.
Through each tear-stained eye
he sees the world
and you.

Jesus said, "Abide in me.
as I abide in you."
When those about us come
to seek the Lord,
will they find him in us?
Have we made him a home in our lives
where others can meet him?

Lent 6 • Palm Sunday
Mark 1:1-11

When trave'ling to Jerusalem
they came to Bethany.
Th' apostles were instructed
a tethered colt to free
and bring for Him to ride upon
though it had not been trained.
They said, "The Lord has need of it,"
when those nearby complained.
Hosanna, Hosanna, let everybody sing
Hosanna, Hosanna, Hosanna to our King.

They brought the colt to Jesus
and upon it laid a cloak
and Jesus sat upon it.
There were others there who broke
the branches from the trees
and, in his path, they laid them out.
Then, forming a procession,
as they walked they raised a shout.
Hosanna, Hosanna, let everybody sing
Hosanna, Hosanna, Hosanna to our King.

They sang, "We praise Jehovah for
the one who, in his name,
is bringing us the kingdom,
prosperity and fame.
The crowd was very happy
and they made the heavens ring.
'Twas quite a celebration
as they'd march along and sing:
Hosanna, Hosanna, let everybody sing
Hosanna, Hosanna, Hosanna to our King.

We too, all sing Hosanna,
as we celebrate the day
the Lord came to the city
in that great triumphal way.
We speak of the procession
and we make a happy scene.
Did you ever stop to wonder,
when you say it, what you mean?
Hosanna, Hosanna, let everybody sing
Hosanna, Hosanna, Hosanna, to our King.

Palm Sunday

(Roman Catholic)

Matthew 26:14-66

Whoever first put up a cross
and hung a man thereon,
was in the devil's service
in a lofty echelon.

For torture was his motive
as his victim surely found
beginning with the moment
he was laid upon the ground
and iron nails were driven
through his wrists into the tree,
a torture, in itself, enough
to fill eternity.

The joints were pulled; the body torn;
the cross was stained with blood
when deep into its socket hole
it dropped with cruel thud.
Then, hanging there in torment,
every limb would rack with pain,
with mouth as dry as desert
bringing fire to the brain.

Such death upon a cross
is truly diabolical,
which makes the power of God to shine
whenever I recall
that God could take the devil's cross
and make a sign of love
that lifts us, not to torment
but to heavenly realms above.

Sunday of the Passion
Mark 14:15-47

In the shadows of the garden
kneels the darker shadow yet
of a man upon his knees
in agony of bloody sweat.
As he kneels, a bloody specter,
mocking, comes before his eyes
of a cruel Roman cross to
torment him in his demise.

In humility he prays with such
a heart afflicted plea,
"Father, if it be Thy will,
remove this suffering from me."
Yet the ending of his prayer
reflects the faithful, loving Son
as he ends his pained petition
saying, "Let Thy will be done."

Sunday of the Passion
Mark 14:15-47

All the depths of human anguish
came that hour to combine
with the great redeeming pow'r of
sacrificial love divine.
How the angels must have wept
to hear that agonizing cry,
knowing well that human sin
required him that death to die.

To you and me a garden is
a very happy place
where God's creative genius
puts on such a happy face.
But Jesus was not there to hear
the birds or see the flowers.
His human life was ebbing
in the face of human powers.
In our own post-resurrection world
we really can't conceive
of the sadness in the garden
on that first Good Friday Eve.

Good Friday

(Alternative)

John 19:17-30

Is it nothing to you that He hung on the cross?
Is it nothing to you who pass by,
That he hung there in pain and in torment to die,
that our gain would be great as his loss?

Is it nothing to you that he died there in shame
that our lives might with glory be filled,
that alone and rejected by men he was killed,
as he prayed to relieve them of blame?

Is it nothing to you that the darkness of death
came the light of the world to dispel,
And that death into darkest oblivion fell
as creation itself held its breath?

It is nothing to you that he could not be held
by the grave which is other men's end?
It's a promise that we who know him as a friend
have our terror of dying dispelled.

Is it nothing to you that the fear of the grave
need no longer put life in its shade?
For the price of our sin, by the Christ has been paid
on that cross where he suffered to save.

HE IS RISEN

He is risen. He is risen!
Hear the women cry.
John and Peter ran together,
saw where He did lie.
There the linen cloths were folded
that had wrapped Him round,
otherwise the tomb was empty.
Hear their joyful sound:
He is risen. He is risen.
Christ is risen indeed.
Down through countless ages,
Christians have agreed.
Jesus Christ is risen and
from death He has been freed.

So join me now with all the saints
of Christiandom and say,

"He is risen. He is risen.
Jesus Christ is risen today."

Easter Day

(Alternative)

Mark 16:1-8

It's Easter Day, a day of joy,
a time to celebrate,
a time to count our blessings
as in church we congregate.

But, Lord, amid the joys I feel,
I have some questions too.
Some things I just don't understand.
So I must ask of you:

Lord, how can life begin with death
and love from hate be born?
How can a gift be made of this:
a corpse, by nails torn?

How can we call a Friday Good
that sees such torture wrought?
How can the future of our race
by mortal pain be bought?

Mark 16:1-8

What a bunch of silly women!
Such a foolish tale they tell!
Seems the happenings of Friday
put them under quite a spell.
They are having foolish visions,
seeing Jesus everywhere.
Maybe it's their tears that make it
hard to see just who is there.

Even though they saw the Master
dying there upon the cross,
now they think they see him living.
Maybe they can't stand the loss.
Women are such frail creatures,
seeing things that are not real.
Grief has made them lose their senses;
I can see how they must feel.

Simon Peter's going fishing,
gone with Andrew, James and John.
They can't spend much time in weeping.
Life, for them, must carry on.
Each of us is filled with sorrow.
Still we have to face the fact.
Now that we have lost our Leader
none of us know how to act.

Silly thought, I almost wish that
what the women say was true.
It would change the world forever
and our faith in God renew.
Maybe we should go and see if
something's really happening
and replace the dreams of women
with men's solid reasoning.

Easter Day, B

Andrew Daughters

How can a King be crowned with thorns,
and on a cross enthroned?
What kind of love was his who there
for human sin atoned?

How could he ask forgiveness
for his murderers that day?
How could he think of others
as his life's blood ebbed away?

And yet, somehow, as I look back
on Easter Day, I see
those thorns become a halo
and those scarred hands blessing me!

Easter 2
John 20:19-31

There is a kind of doubt that
I see often evidenced.
It finds out just what you believe,
and that's what it's against.
It challenges authority
of every kind there is
and will accept no other's
as proper, only his.
I find it hard to live with.
It's exhausting. I confess.
When I was young it had a name.
We called it 'orneriness.'

Another kind of doubt there is
that opens not its eyes
for fear some new disturbing facts
might take it by surprise.
So proudly it proceeds through life
as smug as it can be,
as though it had the answer to
all Godly mystery.

This kind of doubt is sometimes found
within the church's walls,
as though we'd reached perfection.
The very thought appalls.
More often though, it seems to me
I find this kind of doubt
most prevalent among the folk
who are much less devout.

A kind of doubt there is that is
a seeking for the truth.
It typifies the scientist,
the seeker and the sleuth.
It looks for clues and follows them,
persisting in the search
until it finds an answer.
It is sometimes found in church.
It seems to me to be the kind of
doubt that Thomas had.
And, if you think of it that way,
It's really not so bad.

How slow was the walk to Emmaus!
How fast do they run in return!
And between the two trips, what excitement.
To tell it, their lips fairly burn.

"We have been with the Lord." they are crying.
"We have seen Him alive." they exclaim.
"In the breaking of bread, we perceived Him.
Though He died, He's alive!" they proclaim.

Then they told how their hearts burned within them
as the prophecies made them aware.
But they hardly had finished their witness,
when the Lord Himself stood with them there.

And He said to them, "Peace be upon you.
Do not fear. It is I, not a ghost.
See my hands and my feet. You may touch me."
For their hearts filled with fear uppermost.

There's a lesson or two we could learn here,
as we think of those men on that day.
When we witness to Jesus in our lives,
He may come in among us and stay.

So, when two or three gather together
and the Lord, as He promised, is here,
then the threats of the world aren't important.
He has conquered the world and its fear.

Easter 4
John 10:11-18

Have you seen the sheep that graze
in thousands on the western hills?
They feed there as a scattered flock.
Then, suddenly, gathering, they move
like small, wind driven wisps of cloud,
which, when gathered,
pour bleating down the slopes.
And each bleat is a loud complaint
directed at the dogs,
those marvels of obedience who,
following the herder's call,
or word, or hand or whistle,
run busily about,
butting, nipping, barking
and so compel them to come in.

But these are sheep without a shepherd.
They know no voice. They come not at a call.
They hardly know the herdsman
whose will controls their lives.
And they are moved by fear, not love.
They are not led but driven.

Have you ever seen a shepherd
who leads his flock?
He gathers them about him with his words.
His dogs are there only to guard.
The shepherd knows each sheep from all the rest.
And they will follow where he leads,
to pasture and to water,
to shelter and to rest.

So what then is the difference
'Twixt sheep-herder and shepherd?
The force that moves the sheep,
the threat'ning teeth or calling voice,
the fear of dogs or faith in shepherd.

And what moves your life, my friend?
Are you led by the Shepherd or driven
by the dogs of life?

Easter 5
John 15:1-8

Pears and apples,
plums and peaches
all are fruits our God inspires.
Love and mercy,
Jesus teaches
are the fruits His love requires.

Figs and cherries,
nuts and berries,
trees and vines identify.
Charity that
never varies,
God's disciples classify.

Thoughtfulness and
hope and beauty,
these, will loving hearts produce.
Cheerfulness
fulfilling duty
never needs to make excuse.

All the virtues
seen in giving
respite from our human strife,
these, the fruits
of Christian living
decorate the vine of life.

Jesus Christ,
the Vine Divine
is reaching out to all the earth.
We, His branches
intertwine
with all the world to bring new birth.

Easter 5

(Episcopal)
John 14:15-21

Jesus promised he would send us
one who'd love us and befriend us,
God's own Spirit to protect us,
and on Christ's own path direct us.

Holy Spirit stands beside us,
here to strengthen and to guide us.
With his aid our souls are stronger,
and withstand temptation longer.

Help us now to know his presence,
who of God is very essence.
Let us worship and adore him.
Let us thank our savior for him.

Lord, you have not left us friendless.
In your love so strong and endless,
you have more than kept your promise.
Never take your spirit from us.

The comforter he sent is one
by whom our strength is built,
not just an aid to quiet rest,
a soft and downy quilt.

The strength he brings is not there just
for contest or for show.
It's given for the helping up
of those who've fallen low.

Easter 6
John 15:9-17

What a wondrous companion is Jesus,
who has called me to come as his friend.
He has promised to be with me always,
and to stand by me, world without end.

In his presence is peace everlasting.
And with him I'm secure as can be.
For I know that no evil can harm me.
And from fear I shall always be free.

When I talk with him he always hears me
and I know that he cares how I feel.
So with him I can dare to be open
and my innermost thoughts I reveal.

Just to know he is always beside me
brings me joy that just can't be expressed.
So together we do many errands
and I see many lives he has blest.

And whenever I might disappoint him
or have done what he cannot approve,
he will always forgive me completely
and welcome me back to his love.

It was Jesus who made this arrangement.
It was Jesus who chose me as friend.
So I know I shall cherish him always
and follow him through to the end.

When my life comes at last to completion
and they lay my remains neath the sod,
I can think of no finer inscription
than that, "Here lies a friend of his God."

Ascension Day
Luke 24:44-53

"How poor we are," said Matthew,
"In this world where richness counts."
Said Jesus, "Give to all the world
in widening amounts."

"How weak we are," said Thomas.
"No power at all have we."
Said Jesus, "Change the world
and set the people in it free."

"How few we are," said Peter.
"How can we do anything?"
Said Jesus, "You are numbered
with the angels God will bring."

How fearful the disciples were,
Exploited and downtrod.
Said Jesus, "Witness to the world
the mighty power of God."

When you are feeling helpless,
weak and poor and powerless,
Remember who is with you.
He will strengthen you and bless.

For Jesus said, "I'm with you.
I will guard you and defend."
Today that still is true and
always will be to the end.

Ascension Day

(Roman Catholic)
Mark 16:15-20

Only twelve were called,
only twelve.
Fishermen, a tax collector and such,
simple men,
common men they were,
called by a carpenter.

Braggart, doubter, deserter,
fearful men they were,
impulsive, undependable,
sometimes cowardly.
And yet they changed the world.

What are your faults?
They are many.
I know them well.
They are mine.

And yet — perhaps,
if we hear our call,
and follow — together,
we, too, can change the world.

Jesus prayed for us, my brothers,
asked that we might all be one.
Jesus prayed for us, my sisters,
May his holy will be done.

May we learn to love each other
as he prayed that we might do.
Let us strive to work together
our commitment to renew.

Let us learn to pray together
that his will may come to pass.
Let us pray for one another,
that in love we might surpass.

Jesus asked for these things for us
so that we might know his joy
in our hearts in all its fullness,
that no evil could destroy.

So, my brothers and my sisters,
let us all who know his prayer
ask the Lord to work within us,
all his love and work to share.

Let us ask the Lord to use us
as we go forth in his name,
reaching out to one another
and, for him his world to claim.

Pentecost
John 15:26-27, 16:4b-15

Come, Holy Spirit.
Come, Holy Guide.
Teach me to follow and turn not aside.

Come, Holy Spirit.
Come, Holy Fire.
Burn into ashes each unclean desire.

Come, Holy Spirit.
Come, Holy Wind,
you, my forgiveness each time I have sinned.

Come, Holy Spirit.
Spirit and soul,
enter me; strengthen me; making me whole.

Come, Holy Spirit.
Come, Holy Breath.
Fill me with peace at the hour of my death.

Come, Holy Spirit
with hallowing strength.
Lead me to heaven, my homeland, at length.

Pentecost

(Lutheran)
John 7:37-39a

Holy Spirit, Living Water,
flowing from the Father's throne,
Wash us clean in mind and motive,
Help us live for you alone.
Fill us with your perfect presence.
Strengthen us to do your will.
Guide us in our life together.
In our hearts, your love fulfill.

Different gifts you bring among us,
that together we may grow.
Teach us how to work together
that your fullness we may know.

Holy Spirit, you have led us
to the waters of new birth.
Send us as your chosen vessels
to the thirsty of the earth.
Flowing through the hearts of others,
loving spirit, you have come.
Flow through us as willing channels,
filling all of Christendom.

Pentecost

(Roman Catholic and Episcopal)
John 20:19-23

Jesus said to his apostles,
"Peace be with you, peace.
and if there are doubts within you,
let all doubting cease."
When they saw his hands and side,
they knew that it was he.
Then their joy escaped all bounds
and glad they were and free.

"Peace be with you," once again
he said, to break the spell.
"As my Father sent me forth,
I send you forth as well."
Breathing then his spirit on them
Jesus said, "Receive.
Now is Holy Spirit with you.
This you can believe:
Those whose sins you have forgiv'n,
will find their sure release
and those whose sins you shall retain
will find no real peace."

What an awesome burden he has
given us who bear his name:
that the world should know forgiveness
and from whom forgiveness came.
God wants everyone forgiven,
brought again to know his love.
You and I must share the message
of forgiveness from above.

You and I, who know the good news
may not keep it for ourselves.
We must never keep the faith
tucked way up on our inner shelves.
For our faith, if great or little,
though we think we've none to spare,
there's just one way to increase it.
That's to give it out, to share.

Trinity Sunday
John 3:1-17

Nicodemus said to Jesus,
"How can such things ever be?
How can I be born again
when I am over forty-three?
How can I return again
into my mother's womb?
How can I go back again
when halfway to the tomb?

But Jesus said to Nicodemus,
"Don't you understand?
And yet you are a leader of
the Jews in all the land!
The flesh has given birth to flesh.
But on the other hand,
the spirit brings forth spirit,
just as my Father planned."

"And there is much that God has done,
and more that he will do.
If earthly things are past your mind,
then heav'nly things are too.
As Moses lifted up the snake,
when in the wilderness,
so will the Son of Man be
lifted up that he may bless."

Lord, I'm like Nicodemus
and I just don't understand
how God can do the things he does
nor know what he has planned.
It's quite beyond my intellect,
enough to make me frown.
So, help my faith to pick me up
when brainpow'r lets me down.

And Lord, I thank you that you made
the test for heav'n contain
more measure of the human heart
than of the human brain.

Trinity Sunday

(Roman Catholic)
Matthew 28:16-20

If I should tell you, "In the air
above the western hills,
the sky is laced with cloud and smog,
'twould hardly give you thrills."
If I should say, "The evening sun,
refracted and dispersed,
has shortened up its wave-lengths
as in clouds it is immersed,

Would analyzing such as that
bring happiness to you,
or wouldn't it be better
just to share the sunset view?
So Jesus didn't analyze
who He was called to be.
He just told those who spoke to Him
that they should, "Come and see."

So often we theologize
and think we must impress
in fancy terms about the Lord
the people we would bless.
Our words may demonstrate our wit
and make a crafty show,
but Jesus' love was meant to share,
just like the sunset's glow.

Said Jesus, "Go to all the world
and teach what you've been taught.
And share with people everywhere
the vision you have caught."
So don't think clever speech will
win disciples everywhere.
Just show the love for God and man
that you and Jesus share.

So many laws, ancient and modern,
All are important, someone is sure.

In North Carolina,
Thou shalt plow no cotton field with an elephant.

In Victorian England,
Speak ill of the Queen and become an Australian.

In Maryland,
Thou shalt hold thy nose for not over a second.

In Hawaii,
Thou shalt put no pennies into thine ears.

In Kentucky,
Thou shalt walk no public road in a bathing suit
unless thou carryest a club.

In Jesus' time,
Thou shalt pick no grain to eat on the Sabbath,
even if hungry.

How important?
I wonder.

More important,
how important to God?

Jesus questioned.

(All laws quoted are genuine.)

Jesus said, "A house divided
cannot stand. It soon must fall.
And a kingdom torn asunder
comes to nothing good at all."

Lord, I see so many people
all at odds within the soul.
As they cannot serve two masters,
they have trouble being whole.

All divided as to purpose,
serving God and Mammon too,
their priorities are scattered
and their loyalties askew.

Sometimes I too am divided,
wanting heav'n, yet tied to earth.
Half my heart is your dominion.
Half reflects my mortal birth.

Only you can make me whole, Lord.
Only you can make me one.
Heal me. Make me undivided,
just as you are with your son.

Help me get myself together,
my priorities in place.
So, when comes my time for dying,
I, at last shall see your face.

Did you ever notice, as I think I have,
how the great, important sounding words
have so little effect upon our lives?

Words like 'antidisestablishmentarianism,"
or 'librocubicularist' or even
'supercalifragilisticexpialidosius'
hardly change my life at all.

But the little words,
the simple words
can change my life forever!

Words like 'love,'
words like 'hate,'
words like 'live,'
words like 'die,'
these small words in simple phrases
lift me up or lay me low.

'I love you.'
'He will live,'
make my day, my week, my life.

'I hate you.'
'I will leave.'
'She will die.'
These are great earthshaking statements.
They can crack my life's foundations
and topple the walls of my security.

'God loves me.'
'Help me, Lord.'
These small cries are the keys
to the storehouse where lie
all the healing balms of heaven.

In the hardest days of living
they give courage to continue
and strength as I rebuild.

Jesus, come and take my tiller,
for my boat is very small.
And the wind is growing stronger
and the waves are very tall.

As the fishermen were anxious
in the storm on Galilee,
I am filled with fear and panic
and the future threatens me.

Toxic wastes in food and water,
threaten every living form.
Poisoned air and radiation,
these are my surrounding storm.

Angry men in stupid actions
taking hostage innocents
are expanding our supply of
vicious hate and violence.

Must there be another conflict,
mushroom cloud and fiery blast?
Are we bound for Armegeddon?
Is the time for living past?

Waken, Lord, and still the waters.
Bid the winds of anger cease.
Rouse our faith and calm our spirits.
Help us, Lord, to live in peace.

Jairus was a proud man,
Not just one in a crowd man.
He had a lot of power.
So he had no need to cower.
Yet, he knelt before the Lord.

For Jairus had a daughter
who filled his heart with laughter.
She was his pride and pleasure,
his only child and treasure,
her love, his golden hoard.

When she came down with sickness
then with unexpected meekness,
Jairus knelt before the Master
and, afraid of this disaster,
asked for help that she might live.

Jesus took her by the hand then
and commanded her to stand. When
she stood up, he said to feed her,
which was now her only need. Were
any gift more great to give?

Jesus never seemed to panic.
No human power nor Satanic
swerved his calm determination
to effect our restoration
to his presence and his way.

It seems, when things look hopeless,
that I always seem to cope less
satisfactorily than ever;
Lord, so grant that I may never
all my love for you betray.

Proper 9 • Pentecost 7 • Ordinary Time 14
Mark 6:1-6

"We knew him when," the people cried.
"We saw him grow to manhood.
We saw him help his father as
each diligent young man would.
Where does he get the notion
that he has a right to speak thus?
How could he be a prophet, come
from God on high to seek us?"

"He speaks as with authority.
He speaks as one with answers.
We can't believe a carpenter
is one of life's dispensers."
And so his hometown turned away.
They put no faith in Jesus.
So he did no great work there,
though elsewhere he'd be famous.

Proper 9 • Pentecost 7 • Ordinary Time 14
Mark 6:1-6

Do we, perhaps, the selfsame thing,
who've known of him since childhood?
For we don't get excited now
as someone in the wild would.
For us, Good News, no longer new
has somehow lost its flavor.
Or are we so accustomed that
we've lost our will to savor?

And yet, my friends, do not lose hope.
The Father's love is boundless.
And if our faith is but lukewarm,
at least it is not groundless.
Perhaps, if God can those forgive
who've railed at him and ranted,
He may forgive us, even us
who take him so for granted.

Proper 10 • Pentecost 8 • Ordinary Time 15
Mark 6:7-13

When Jesus called a dozen
from the field and shop and shore,
they all rose up and followed,
were with him a year or more.
By parables he taught them,
how his Father's kingdom was.
They were learning as they watched him
heal the sick and leperous.

But the time came when, no longer
did he tell them only, "Come."
He also told them, "Go and heal
the blind, the deaf and dumb."
He sent them out to preach and
call the people to repent.
And, two and two together,
they went out as they were sent.

Things are really not much different
from the way they were of old.
We are called to be disciples
and to *follow* we are told.
But we're also told to, *"Go"*
And call the peoples to repent
for the healing of the nations
as the first apostles went.

We are called, not just to "keep the faith."
Instead, we're called to share.
And we find the more we give away,
the more we have to spare.
So let us be disciples,
called to *follow* Jesus' word.
And let us also *go* and be
apostles of the Lord.

The sheep has been domesticated
for so many years,
that a sheep without a shepherd
can succumb to many fears.
When his wool is long and heavy
and he's lying on a hill,
if his feet are up the slope,
he cannot stand. He never will.

Sheep aren't really very bold and
they are also not too bright.
While they seldom do much thinking,
they are easy to excite.
If a flock should start to panic
and a leader should arise,
foolishly, they all will follow
though it lead to their demise.

Take a look at human hist'ry.
You will find we're much like sheep.
People sometimes follow leaders
like they're walking in their sleep.
Let a Fuhrer or a Duce
or an Ayatollah come
who will play upon their fears
and thinking turns to minimum,
which makes a very fertile place for
bigotry and animus.
And that's why we need a shepherd
who will rescue us from us.

Mother, you could never guess.
It's a miracle, no less.
Five small loaves and two small fish
served a multitude to nourish.

When you let me go today
up into the hills to play,
there I heard a rabbi teach.
Thousands came to hear him preach.

But, when noontime came along,
everything was going wrong.
Not a soul in all that bunch
seemed to think to bring a lunch.

When I offered them my sack,
one man said he'd take me back
to the man who'd spoken there
if I had some lunch to share.

Rabbi made them all sit down
right out there upon the ground,
Blest and fed the multitude
with my little bag of food.

Afterwards he had them fill
many baskets on that hill
with the leftovers they had.
I was one astonished lad.

Mother, only God could do
something like I'm telling you.
Now, one thing sure puzzles me.
Who can that man Jesus be?

Proper 12

(Episcopal)
Mark 6:45-52

Jesus came across the water
as th' apostles rowed in vain,
for the wind and waves about them
cancelled most of every gain.

When they saw him, they were fearful,
told each other, "It's a ghost."
But he spoke and reassured them,
quieted their fears, almost.

As he climbed into their vessel,
calm the winds became and hushed.
They were sore amazed and wondered
and their countenances flushed.

Was he walking? Was he swimming?
Were his sandals wet or dry?
Some may wonder how he got there.
I'm more interested in, "Why?"

Did he float above the water?
Did he leap from wave to wave?
I'm more interested in knowing
that he came his friends to save.

I believe, if God had wanted,
Jesus could have walked the sea.
But I don't find that important,
not today, to you and me.

What I do find is important
is the fact this story shows.
When his friends are deep in trouble,
Jesus somehow always knows.

Miracles don't really matter,
hardly trouble me at all.
What's important is the knowing,
Jesus comes whene'er I call.

When the Israelites wandered for years
in the wilderness, haunted by fears,
knowing not where at last they would go,
They knew not how to get there. And so
they just followed the way they were led
by the fire and the cloud. And were fed
by the hand all unseen from above.
That's how they learned of God and his love.

When the multitudes followed the Lord
O'er the lake to be taught by his word,
they grew hungry and then they were fed
with some fish and a few loaves of bread.
But both Moses and Jesus soon found
that as long as the food would abound
they had followers more than can tell.
When the food went, the crowd would dispel.

And what will be said about us?
When we get what we want, we don't fuss.
But when we're disappointed, we pout.
And we wonder what prayer's all about.
So the question perhaps we should ask,
"Is our faith real, or is it a mask?
Is there faith in the way that I live
or do I just want what God can give?"

"Do I follow the Lord for himself?
or would I follow just any old elf
who'd allow me ten wishes to make?
Do I really have faith or a fake?
Are God's gifts more important to see
than the Lord is who gives them to me?
If my faith's just a means and a tool,
tell me, 'Whom do I think I can fool?' "

Questions, questions, always questions,
Most of them begin with, "How?"
Much as our own daily questions
of the Lord are prefaced now.
"Tell us how, Lord; we will do it.
We will take it on from there.
We don't need your presence in it.
We can make life good and fair."

If the Lord had felt that "how to"
was the most important thing,
he'd have sent a "how to" manual
down to teach us everything.
But, instead, he sent us Jesus.
Maybe we should ask him "Why?"
Why should God have sent us Jesus
here to teach and live and die.

Proper 14 • Pentecost 12 • Ordinary Time 19

John 6:35, 41-51

Maybe it's because there is no
"how to" book to teach us love,
how to learn to love each other
as the Lord does up above.
It is only by example
we can learn to love at all.
That's the lesson man has needed
ever since before the fall.

Jesus gave us that example.
Jesus taught us how to give,
not by diagram or concept.
He just showed us how to live,
How to live for one another.
And if we will hear his call,
we can live an Alleluia
to the God who loves us all.

Proper 15 • Pentecost 13 • Ordinary Time 20
John 6:51-58

Lord, you just don't make it easy
when you say to follow you,
so your churches are not crowded
and your followers are few.

For there's some of what you said
that's hard for people to accept.
Some of it divides your people.
Some is easy to reject.

Take for instance, "Eat my body,
Drink my blood." That's what you said.
Most of those who heard you say it
turned away from where you led.

Lord, you knew that they'd have problems
thinking of your flesh as food.
And you knew that Jews would boggle
at the thought of drinking blood.

Almost seems to me you had
a plan to drive them all away.
Seems almost as though you wanted
only just the twelve to stay.

I can think of no way better
you could earn their enmity.
Almost seems to me you planned
to send yourself to Calvary.

Many folks had left the Lord
when his mighty claim they heard:
that his father'd sent him out,
brand new life to bring about.

They would not believe his claim
that, as bread of life he came,
words of life to bring to them,
their eternal death to stem.

Jesus turned then to the twelve,
asked them in their hearts to delve,
asked if they would leave him too
as the others all would do.

This time Peter spoke up well.
He wished not to say farewell.
He'd stay with Jesus; reason is
that the words of life are his.

Proper 16 • Pentecost 14 • Ordinary Time 21
John 6:55-69

"Lord, you have the words of life,
words to put an end to strife,
words to show us how to love,
how to think like God above."

Lord, like Peter I would be,
looking toward eternity,
learning how to live each day,
following in Jesus' way.

•   •   •

Help me speak the words you spoke
as your presence I invoke.
Let the words of living flow
straight through me to all I know.
Help me make the words I speak
fit the kind of life I seek.
So, when heaven's hymns are sung,
they won't seem a foreign tongue.

Proper 17 • Pentecost 15 • Ordinary Time 22
Mark 7:1-8, 14-15, 21-23

Lord, there are times you threaten me
as I think what you know
of what goes on inside of me
when I am high or low.
When I am seething deep inside
but on the surface, calm,
my smile can fool most every one.
With them, I have no qualm.

With them, it's easy to conceal
what's happening within.
But you know all my cussedness
and all my secret sin.
It's pretty hard to realize
that you know more of me
than I will know about myself
until eternity.

You know all my hypocrisies.
You're quick to point them out.
But, when you do, I'm grateful
that you whisper. You don't shout.
Let's keep it confidential, Lord.
If everybody knew
the things you know about me,
then my friends would number few.

So please be patient with me, Lord.
and give me many days
with hope that somehow I'll improve
and follow in your ways.
And please, Lord, as you judge each day,
just don't let me forget
that I'm still incomplete, 'cause
you aren't finished with me yet.

Lord, we all have a measure of deafness,
though our ears may perform very well
and we also may suffer from dumbness,
though our words tumble out pell mell.

But our deafness is very selective.
There are some things we seem to ignore.
We may hear a concerto by Mozart,
but not the distress of the poor.

We are mute in the face of injustice
just as long as our own rights are safe.
We protest not the bondage of others
if their bonds don't compel us to chafe.

Lord, if we don't pay you much attention,
Well, I guess that it's really not odd.
If we can't hear the voices of people,
should we hear the still small voice of God?

Hello, my friend, you really look down
with your back all bent and face in a frown.
That cross that you carry is really a load.
You're not making much progress along the road.

And what is this burden upon my back?
It feels so heavy, my back may crack.
Sometimes I think I can hardly move.
I struggle along. But what do I prove?

What's that, you say? Will I give you a hand
when I'm so weighted down I can hardly stand?
And you don't need help as badly as I.
But if you'll help me, let's give it a try.

O my! That's better. My strength is back.
How are you so strong as to lift my pack?
Look. Now I can stand with my back up straight
and, to tell the truth, I feel just great.

And that burden you carry seems lighter, my friend.
Though it still looks heavy, you hardly bend.
You stand so straight and walk so tall,
One would hardly notice your cross at all.

And isn't it strange how that worked out?
When we help each other, we both feel stout
as though we got help when our backs were sore
from Someone who's carried a cross before.

When I think of the child who was held that day,
held in the arms of the Lord,
then I wonder how much, in his childish way,
he perceived or was he bored.

He was placed in the midst of a group of men
at the center of all their eyes
to be made an example in teaching them
their calling to recognize.

Sometimes I wish I had been that child
and had known Him as I know now.
I'd have treasured each word, every time He smiled,
every lift of that thoughtful brow.

Had that child but known whose arms were those
that held him in love so dear,
he'd have wanted to stay in that safe repose
with the Master forever near.

And yet, dear friends, if we only knew,
down deep in our heart and soul,
His arms await us. Yes, friends, it's true.
And He'll lift us and make us whole.

But we often squirm and wriggle away
from those arms where we're safe and sure,
like a child who would much rather go and play.
Our own will has so great a lure.

Lord, help us to know that our hope depends
(wherever our way is trod,)
on a life that's lived and a life that ends
in the arms of a loving God.

Proper 21 • Pentecost 19 • Ordinary Time 26
Mark 9:38-50

The apostles were not very happy one day,
the result of what they saw as danger,
for someone had cured in the name of the Lord
who was not one of them, but a stranger.

But Jesus, when they had complained to him, said,
"Let him be. And be not so suspicious.
And always remember, if you would have peace,
he who is not against us is with us."

Proper 21 • Pentecost 19 • Ordinary Time 26
Mark 9:38-50

What a lesson that day, the apostles had learned
and it's one that we often still need
if we really would grow in the love of the Lord
and from arrogance we would be freed.

It is hard to remember that God is not ours
and is not our own private possession.
Rather quite the reverse, we belong to the Lord
and we ought to learn this in addition:

If our movement is slow when we act in his name
or our zeal for his will should diminish,
God is perfectly capable, when there is need,
to use others, his will to accomplish.

And the whole truth of God is too vast to be known.
Now, if all of mankind cannot fathom,
then how foolish it is for one man to lay claim
that he comprehends God in His wisdom.

I may well disagree with a fellow I meet
and may think him as wrong as can be,
but he may have some inkling of truth that I need.
And the Christ died for him as for me.

Proper 22 • Pentecost 20 • Ordinary Time 27
Mark 10:2-16

How right he was when Jesus said,
"The two shall be as one,"
when there's a real marriage
and the Father's will is done.

For then there is commitment
on the part of man and wife
to working out the problems
that come into every life.

We find that joy is doubled
when, in love it can be shared
and troubles cut in half
so their full burden can be spared.

And in a real marriage,
there is more that can be said
of the way we grow together
and the way our souls are fed.

Proper 22 • Pentecost 20 • Ordinary Time 27

Mark 10:2-16

I would hope for every couple
they would find before the end
that the one whom each has married
is the very truest friend.

For when there is a failure
in the marriage bond, you see,
there is pain for both the members
in that nuptial surgery.

Even though in total silence
or in anger strong and clear
disappointment may be covered
at the loss of hope so dear.

So when I see a wedding,
for each couple I will pray
that God, somehow will lead them
so that always they can say

That in all their life together
they are truly now as one
And the two they were is smaller
then the one they have become.

Proper 23 • Pentecost 21 • Ordinary Time 28
Mark 10:17-30

Lord, I almost wish you hadn't
said the words you said that day,
how it would be hard for those with
wealth to climb the heavenly way.
For the people you were seeing
had so little when compared
with what I just take for granted
in the worldly things I've shared.

I've a home, a place more comfortable
then any you had seen.
And I probably live better than
the average King or Queen
lived when you were on the earth and
teaching people what to do.
Yet we think that we don't have enough
though real wants are few.

We own things that were not dreamed of.
We enjoy them every day.
And they make our lives so easy.
Yet we seldom think to pray
in thanksgiving for the much we have
we don't appreciate.
And that's too bad. For if we did
then we would really celebrate.

But, at least, Lord, I am grateful
that you said it's not for us,
in the end, to earn our heaven.
I would never make it thus.
Though a rich man can't buy heaven,
still according to your word,
as a gift he can receive it,
like a poor man, from the Lord.

• • •

Lord, when I am taken home,
I know that I can only take
what my lifeless hands can carry
as that final trip I make.
Help me, Lord, convert my treasure
into heaven's currency.
That way, I won't be a pauper
when this life is gone from me.

James and John were fishermen,
the sons of Zebedee.
They left their nets and followed
from the shores of Galilee.

One day they took the Lord aside
and asked of him a boon.
Their wish was understandable
but hardly opportune.

They wanted him to promise
that when he to glory came,
he'd seat them close on either hand,
that they might share the same.

How little did they realize
just what it was to ask.
His glory was no easy road,
but life-consuming task,

To be immersed, as Jesus was,
in earthly stress and pain
and drain his cup of bitter gall,
rejection and disdain.

Had they but known, I really doubt
that they'd have felt it loss
to be denied to share with him
whose glory was a cross!

Blind Bartimaeus, hearing Jesus pass,
let out a shout,
"You Son of David, pity me
for you can help me out."

He asked not for a beggar's gift
of gold or other coin,
but rather, for the gift of sight
that others he might join.

Then Jesus spoke and said to him
in words that would console,
"As you believe that I can heal,
your faith has made you whole."

What joy for Bartimaeus then
was carried in those words.
For then the first face that he saw
was Jesus Christ, the Lord's.

And so, when Jesus started
to Jerusalem again,
this blind man, now no longer blind,
was walking in his train.

Lord, just like Bartimaeus,
we all have our blindness too.
It keeps us all from seeing
what you're wanting us to do.

Lord, take away our blindness
and our prejudice subdue,
so that we, like Bartimaeus,
can walk along with you.

"Love God and love your neighbor."
How simple it would seem
if not for just two problems.
And therein lies my theme.

For loving One so powerful,
with jurisdiction here,
Whose judgment holds my life in hand,
could plainly turn to fear.

To love my neighbor could become
more easy than it is
if he were just more lovable
and saintliness were his.

And then, to make it harder,
when my neighbor comes to view:
the God who says he loves me so,
he loves my neighbor too.

How lucky is my neighbor
His instructions from above:
to love the Lord and also,
I'm the neighbor he's to love.

I guess I'm sort of lucky too.
'Cause what is known to me,
I'll try to hide from him
that I'm as hard to love as he!

Of the people who came to the temple,
there were many whose vesture was grand.
And they came to the Court of the Women
all proudly, with offering in hand.
As they dropped in their gold with a flourish,
that attention of all they would claim.
With their fringes and tassels aswinging,
they might bow to acknowledge their fame.

And then, in a moment of quiet,
in a robe that was ragged and worn,
came a widow, who slipped through the temple
among people who viewed her with scorn.
As she came to the place of the off'ring,
from her pocket, two coppers she took.
And she placed them amidst all the silver
and gold, hoping no one would look.

But One saw, Who sat in the background,
Who knew just how hard it had been
for the widow to put in both coppers
from an income so terribly thin.
Jesus spoke of it to his disciples.
And he told them the gift that she gave
was greater than gold coins or silver,
as nothing she held back to save.

There were many who gave from their plenty,
great gifts of their silver and gold.
But she gave, of her little, the total.
She had nothing left to withhold.
And the value of anything given,
whatever the off'ring may be,
should be seen in its cost to the giver.
He who gave on the cross would agree.

The time of God and that of man
are very different things,
as different as the differences
of cabbages from Kings.
Our God has worked for ages
in fulfillment of his plan,
in contrast to the quick demands
of small impatient man.

Our time, we mark in decades
while, for him the eons fly.
A thousand years for him is
like the blinking of an eye.
Sometimes that brings frustration,
makes us want to scream and shout.
But God's view is the long one and
he knows what he's about.

As he won't rush to judgment
in deciding on our fate,
I guess we should be thankful
that his patience is so great.
Don't fret about his schedule.
Just be glad he's slow to move.
For he will need less time to judge
than we will to improve.

Proper 28

(Episcopal)

Mark 13:14-23

Come follow the Fuhrer
and learn to salute
and to march with a flag and a gun
to a moment of glory
created from fear;
there may be nothing left when you're done.

Though nearly two thousand
long summers have gone,
it is still true as Jesus had said:
there are still many, Christs,
who are burning to lead
and still millions who want to be led.

But there's only one way
to be sure it is Christ,
when the call comes to, "Follow, who may."
For the Christ has not changed
though the ages are long.
He's the same through the years and today.

If the earthly "Messiah"
preach hatred for men
or seek power or riches of fame,
He is hardly the Christ
that we find in our book
and is surely unworthy the name.

So, in choosing a leader,
be careful. Beware!
And don't be too impressed by his speed.
Though it's all very well
to make haste on the way,
more important is where he will lead.

Who knows when it will happen
that the end of time will come?
It seems meaningful to many
and irrelevant to some.

But, should it come while I'm alive,
'Twill come as a surprise.
For no one knows the day or hour
or has the least surmise.

Though many play the numbers game
and think they have the key,
that time is still God's secret
and it ever more shall be.

However, I am not concerned,
for I am well aware,
no matter what some folks may say,
my ignorance they share.

There's really just one answer,
if you really want to know:
and that's to live each day as if
today's the day to go.

Proper 29 • Last Pentecost • Christ the King
John 18:33-37

What kind of a Kingdom has Jesus?
No castle nor palace has he.
No congress nor parliament sitting,
deciding what laws there will be.
Perhaps he has need of but two laws:
Love God and your neighbor as well.
To obey them is all that is needed,
as all of the saintly can tell.

He has neither army nor navy,
no air force to guard the frontiers
to keep out the strangers unwanted
and maintain the enemy's fears.
Immigration he seems to encourage,
of some quite disreputable,
like fishermen, publicans, sinners.
To such he is hospitable.

It seems there's no revenue service
or taxes we must calculate.
He surely cannot run a kingdom
on what we put into the plate!

Proper 29 • Last Pentecost • Christ the King

John 18:33-37

No 1040 form comes in April
to fill out before the fifteenth,
with penalties charged for nonpayment,
beginning upon the sixteenth.

No currency's here with his picture,
no coinage engraved with his name.
and where are the posters and slogans
proclaiming his power and fame?
And I see no trappings of kingship,
no robes made of velvet and fur,
no crown made of gold set with diamonds,
to befit our supreme arbiter.

Jesus said that his kingdom was really
not what Pilate had thought it had been.
It was not of this world. And its glory
was not of the kind to be seen.
For those of us here in his kingdom,
there is one other thing we have known:
of the kingdoms around in his lifetime,
it's the only one left with a throne.

All Saints' Day
John 11:32-44

"Jesus wept." Had he not heard
that big boys never cry?
He wept with Mary as she told
how Lazarus came to die.

He wept with her. His heart was touched
to see her weeping there.
And, as he wept, his weeping said
her sorrow he would share.

He did not say, "Be brave and strong,"
and thus condemn her tears.
He worried not that he was seen
as sharing in her fears.

If Jesus was so sensitive
to Mary's dreadful loss,
I wonder how he bore so well
the torture of the cross.

If Jesus thus could weep and
did not try his tears to hide,
I wonder why we try to keep
our tears of love inside.

And I believe that Jesus weeps
for human anguish known
throughout the world by those in pain.
He makes their pain his own.

If I would then be Christ-like
and would follow in his way,
I too may weep with others
as I share with them today.

All Saints' Day

(Lutheran and Episcopal)
Matthew 5:1-12

A child, when asked, "Just what is a saint?"
looked up at the stained glass above,
and replied that, "A saint is a person who lets
in the light of God's glory and love."

That's not a bad way to define what is shown
by a saint and his purpose on earth.
And if that's really so, then I guess I have known
quite a few in the years since my birth.

Just think of the people you knew as a child,
and those you may know even now.
And think of the ones through whom heaven has smiled,
though no halo encircles the brow.

Is there father or mother who taught you to know
there's a God who will reach out in love
or who set an example and helped you to grow
in your knowledge of heaven above?

Was there teacher or brother or sister or friend
through whom God came to you once, at least?
Through whom faith came alive more than just at the end?
It could even have been through a priest!

There were saints through the ages whose lives were
    renowned
and whose fame is a light to us all.
But there also are more who are saints, still uncrowned
just because their acquaintance is small.

So let's lift our voices in praise of His Name,
for the multitude time can't erase,
for the slightly known saints who will never know fame,
for the blest "also rans" of our race.

Thanksgiving Day

(Episcopal)
Matthew 6:25-33

It's a very nice thing to be thank-full.
When you're full, thanks is easy to say.
But what if you hadn't a turkey
to eat on this Thanksgiving day?

What if there were no yams or potatoes,
no fixings, cranberries and such,
What if there were just barely a little,
Instead of so all-fired much?

Would you then say your thanks to the Father
who provided this bountiful earth,
and gave us so great a share of it
by accident only of birth?

There are those in the African deserts
and in Asia with little to eat
And in India, where there are millions
to whom not being hungry's a treat.

Thanksgiving Day

(Episcopal)
Matthew 6:25-33

When it comes down to real thanksgiving,
remember that part of the word
is that very important word, "giving,"
not just being full of the bird.

There are multitudes here on this planet
who today will have nothing to eat,
who have only a shack for their shelter,
and nothing to wear on their feet.

These poor ones of earth are our sisters
and brothers, all loved by the Lord.
And when we feed them, we feed Jesus.
For that we have Jesus' own word.

So let's have a real thanks giving
and give out of thanks to the One
who gave for our use his creation
and for our salvation, his Son.

Christmas Eve
Luke 2:1-20

It was dark in the hills of Judea
where the shepherds were guarding their sheep.
And the sounds of the night,
to the shepherd's delight,
were of peace and of rest and of sleep.

Then, high o'er the hills of Judea,
like the sun at the peak of the day,
came a marvelous light
and the shepherds in fright,
fell down on the ground in dismay.

And out of the skies of Judea
came a voice saying, "Fear not at all."
Such a wonderful sound
filled the earth all around.
The shepherds looked up at the call.

Then the voice in the skies of Judea
said, "I bring you great tidings of joy
For a Savior is born
to a world that is torn.
He has come as a baby, a boy.

"Go to Bethlehem town in Judea
where you'll find a most wonderful thing.
In a manger laid down
near the inn of the town
is the Christ Child, the Savior, a King."

Then all heaven broke loose in Judea.
The poor shepherds were sorely amazed.
With a rustle of wing,
all the heavens did sing
as the angelic voices were raised.

"All glory to God in Judea
and all praise to Him all through the earth.
And peace among men,
Alleluia, Amen.
Let all people rejoice at His birth."

So they ran through the night in Judea
and they found that the angels sang true
for the glorious light
that shone through the night
was the love of God shining anew.

Christmas Eve
Luke 2:1-20

Through the rest of their lives in Judea,
shepherds wond'ringly spoke of that night
when Judean hills rang
as the angel host sang
and God's glory shone forth in a light.

It is dark in the skies of our city
and no voices from heaven resound.
But that light is still here,
to our lives ever near.
In our hearts it will ever be found.

'Tis that light that has led on our journey
through life and will lead us above
Through the darkness of sin,
led us closer to Him.
'Tis the light of God's glory and love.

Scripture Index